We Live, We Die

Also by Annette Herd and published by Ginninderra Press
Life Will Find You Again

Annette Herd

We Live, We Die

We Live, We Die
ISBN 978 1 76041 507 5
Copyright © text Annette Herd 2018
Cover photo: Annette Herd

First published 2018 by
GINNINDERRA PRESS
PO Box 3461 Port Adelaide 5015 Australia
www.ginninderrapress.com.au

Contents

1895	7
A Garden of Delights	9
Affair	10
Auschwitz	11
Breath	12
Collective	13
Fearless	14
Feeling Slow	15
First Frost	16
First Love	17
Flowers	18
Haikus	19
Honest	22
Hot Summer's Day	23
If You	24
It Is Not Possible	25
It's Complicated	26
It's Time	28
Judas Had a Role to Play	29
Learnt Nothing	30
Leaving Home	31
Lonely	32
Love in the Outback	33
Love is a Coin Flipped Twice	34
My Me	35
My Right	36
Never Mine	37
Phoenix	38
Rich Beyond Belief	39
Saturated	40

Oh Mother of Mine	41
Summer of Disobedience	42
Summertime Wintertime	43
The Constancy of Change	44
The Crime of Ancestry	45
The Cycle of Politics	47
The Life That Could Have Been	48
The Shell of Your Silence	49
The Silence Within	50
This Is How	51
Three Wishes	52
Tree Change	53
Walk Through Doors That Open	54
Walking	55
Who Do You Think You Are	56
Perfect	57
We Live, We Die	58

1895

He was born in 1895 and then they made him join the Great War
which wasn't really all that great especially when you lose your right hand
at the age of nineteen and most of your mates into the bargain
out there in the trenches full of mud and muck and dead parts.

He told me about this bomb going off in enemy territory
and a Frenchman got blown up. An arm came flying over the line
and landed in their section. He didn't make a big deal of it
same as with his hand when it got shot to mush by a French bullet.

He waited behind the lines for a doctor who never came.
So he walked back further to get himself to a field hospital.
After nine hours of holding his bloody hand with his good one
he was past pain and the hand was past saving.

On Christmas Eve somehow no one felt like fighting.
He remembered hearing French blokes sing 'Silent Night'
over the eerie quiet and the icy wind. They joined in
thinking of their loved ones, missing them from far away.

He was just there, like sunshine, and he never talked much
about the war except when it was just him and me at home
and he'd come with a bottle of wine tucked under his right arm
and two glasses in his left hand and we'd settle at the kitchen table.

He never talked much about the Great War and the time after
which can't have been that great really, when you think about it.
There is one picture of him when he came out of hospital
with his stump all bandaged up. I put it in a safe place

to pass on to my kids and tell them about their great-grandfather who was a hero to me, because he made peace with himself and the world. I'm glad we had those times when he told me about the Great War which wasn't all that great. Really.

A Garden of Delights

What we have planted years ago
Is growing strong and tall
It blossoms, blooms, expands and thrives
Within our union's wall.

It is an ever growing field,
A garden of delights,
Shared with inevitable weeds
Of sorrow, pain and fights.

Here we find shelter, respite, peace,
Here we find room to grow
And when the wind blows us about
We simply let it blow.

Now this is not to say there has
Not ever been a doubt.
Yet every well-loved patch of soil
Survives a spell of draught.

My love for you will always be
A precious thing to hold
Until the day when both of us
Have tenderly grown old.

Affair

Must leave behind love's basic lust
That what I love I must destroy
My conscience tells me that I must

Our bond is bound to bite the dust
I better drop the lovely boy
Must leave behind love's basic lust

I'll end it, that is only just
I will be prim, I will be coy
My conscience tells me that I must

Our marriage wheel is stuck with rust
Yet with our vows I should not toy
Must leave behind love's basic lust

I will content myself with crust
I will forget this shameful joy
My conscience tells me that I must

I will renounce his muscled bust
His cheeky smile in my employ
Must leave behind love's basic lust
My conscience tells me that I must

Auschwitz

Cut-off hair
Pulled-out teeth
Ripped-off rings

Spark-less eyes
Corpse-like living
Piled-up dead

Orders given
Orders taken
Orders executed

Heil Hitler
Hollow cause
Holocaust

I read Magda Szubanski's autobiography *Reckoning*. She describes her Polish father as a huge influence in her life. Her visit to Auschwitz with her parents brought back all the memories and pictures of the Third Reich that were a constant companion of my growing up in Germany. It is still a mystery to me why a whole people would succumb to one man's evil delusions.

Breath

Morsels of memories
Feed my awareness
As I am standing on top of Montmartre
On my own this time
No point in scanning
The terraces down to the City of Love.

I can still feel your breath
On my lips
The taste of love and home and family
So cruelly taken
When Paris turned to terror
And you breathed no more.

Not a true story, but the result of a five-word challenge where you have ten minutes to write a poem including five specific words or their derivatives. In this case it was terraces, memory, breathing, family, and morsel.

Collective

It was not me
Who created concentration camps
In the country of my birth.

It was not me
Who hunted homosexuals
And experimented on the disabled.

It was not me
Who refused
To shake Jesse Owens' hand.

My guilt is not personal. I say sorry all the same.

It was not me
Who invaded
My adopted country.

It was not me
Who massacred and stole
Its first occupants.

It was not me
Who trampled on Dreamings
And created nightmares.

My guilt is not personal. I say sorry all the same.

Fearless

Be fearless

Practise your talent for
Kindness
With random abandon.
Healing
The wounds of others
Will make you
Whole
No matter
How scarred your
Heart
May be.

Feeling Slow

I wake up feeling slow.
I languish in the rays of a milky sun.
I ease myself out of bed.

We amble along the beach
Leaving paw and foot prints
In sand so cold
It half freezes my feet.

Over a hot shower
I give into a day of
Doing nothing.

First Frost

First frost in the Barossa.
Foot and paw prints in icing sugar on luminous green lawns.
A glorious winter sun, all light, no warmth.
Ducks greet the day in pairs.

Muffin in his blue coat with the red border bounces over soft ground.
A four-legged teddy bear.
The world he sees through his one eye is good.
He likes winter.

Toby, typical kelpie, badgers me to find a stick
And promptly forgets about it when
Despite his geriatric hips
A flock of galahs needs pulling in line.

I hug one of the old gum trees.
Toby gets jealous.
He thinks all the hugs in the world are exclusively for him.
I fondle his satin ears and search for another stick.

First Love

You were so different
From all the boys I knew.

I fell for you.

You had
A life and a past.

It couldn't last.

Flowers

More powerful than any gun
Are all these flowers here, my son
Laid in respect for those who died
Defying terrorists who tried
To frighten us and make us hate
I promise you they'll meet their fate.

As you are sitting on my knee
I beg you, listen carefully
I hope the seeds my words have sown
Will blossom once you're fully grown
And you will be a man one day
Who has no hateful word to say.

Let every race and creed unite
United we will win the fight
If we agree to walk as one
There will not be a single gun
To threaten or destroy the powers
We have invested in those flowers.

Inspired by the YouTube clip of a father who helps his little son understand what happened in the terrorist attacks in Paris in November 2015

Haikus

Love found once more
In the autumn of life –
Hearts beat like spring.

Holding hands in spring
Holding her hand in autumn –
His ring's vow fulfilled.

Drops from a faucet
One icy pearl at a time –
I thirst for more.

Love has its seasons.
In the seed of creation
Lies its completion.

Her heart spans across
The distance of time and space –
A mother's love endures.

Veterans visit
Anniversary cancelled –
Long wait for Long Tan.

A bin's lid open
I try and close it again –
The wind laughs at me.

Days getting warmer
Washing drying on the line –
A housewife's delight.

Dogs sleeping in the shade
Tails twitching in the heat –
I stay indoors.

Honest

We could be honest with each other
If you were honest with yourself
As long as you decide to smother
Your inner voice and true desire
You're forcing me to stay a liar
Whatever needs to be revealed
Remains unspoken, unaddressed
Whatever needs to be confessed
Is staying close and undercover
And makes me a reluctant lover

Hot Summer's Day

Nothing seems sweeter to me
Than a hot summer's day in the shade of a tree
Serenaded by the sound of an afternoon breeze
A good book and a drink to please
All my senses.

For a sweet afternoon I am free
While I listen to the song of the tree
Accept the gift of a moment to seize
Dull all my worries and ease
All my troubles.

Faced with the fact eventually
That I have to abandon my place by the tree
I leave with a sense that I am deeply blessed
For I know that I have been caressed
By the Great Mother.

If You

        If you   shut shop.

    If you   build walls.

    If you   didn't   hide truths.

    If you   wear masks.

     If you   cut cords.

      I   could

         love   you

             if   you

               let me

It Is Not Possible

I want to stop time.
I want to turn back the clock.
I want today to last forever.
It is not possible.

I want to fight your fights.
I want to open doors.
I want to turn all lights to green.
It is not possible.

I want to keep you safe.
I want to protect you from harm.
I want to watch over your sleep.
It is not possible.

I want to shield you from hurt.
I want to prevent your mistakes.
I want to diffuse your disappointments.
It is not possible.

A mother trusts.
A mother lets go.
A mother loves until the end of days.

It's Complicated

Do you still love me,
she asks him quietly
and takes his hand.
He pulls it away
and tells her straight
that he doesn't know any more.

I know you want more,
but I can't do this 'marry me'
thing. It sounded straight
out of a novel. He quietly
turns and walks away
with a desolate wave of his hand.

She covers her face with her hand
as she wipes more and more
silent tears away.
The question 'why is he doing this to me?'
finds no answer. She is sobbing quietly.
She can no longer stand up straight.

At home she doesn't want to go straight
inside. No ring on the finger of her left hand.
No joyous news whispered quietly
to a friend or two or more.
No 'look at me'.
No 'I am going to move away'.

He promised to take her away.
With her he would walk the straight
and narrow. Just you and me,
he said, and kissed her hand.
I won't get into trouble no more.
Should she fight or take it quietly?

Night descends quietly.
When he rings she puts the phone away.
She doesn't want to hear any more
from him. She goes straight
to bed, lying there with her hand
on her heart. Did he ever love me?

The door opens quietly. He comes straight
to her side. She doesn't move away when he takes her hand.
Don't cry no more, he says. Come with me.

It's Time

Blame
is too heavy to carry.

Shame
is too heavy to carry.

It's time
to step into the light.

Judas Had a Role to Play

If Jesus was supposed to die
Judas had a role to play
Cause and effect
Decisions and their consequences
Never ending cycles
Of start and finish
Moons wax and wane
Tides ebb and flow
Empires rise and fall
Gravity makes choices for us
Are we ever really free?

Learnt Nothing

We gather once a year
To think of the fallen
Deplore war
And pledge peace.

We place flowers
At the foot of statues
To lament the losses
And remember the sacrifices.

We honour the past
In a present
That has changed nothing
And learnt nothing.

Leaving Home

He has had enough of my discipline.
He has had enough of my guidance.
He has had enough of my mothering.

Keen to shed his childhood
Like a snake who has outgrown its skin
He is like a fledgling
Eager to leave the nest and test his wings
Like a young stallion
Ready to run into his own choosing.

Go my boy
With my tears and my blessings.

Be a man.

Lonely

You talk next to me.
But not with me.

You walk next to me.
But not with me.

You sit next to me.
But not with me.

You sleep next to me.
But not with me.

Love in the Outback

What you see
Is what you get
She said
Putting on
Her Rossi boots.

He liked
What he saw
Grabbed his Akubra
And sauntered over
To get it.

Having gone bush a number of times, the directness and no-nonsense attitude to life of the people living in the Outback has always struck me as something rather wonderful. Life is too short for pretence.

Love is a Coin Flipped Twice

What else is love, but hatred in disguise,
For love demands as much attention as does hate.
What's love to me is hatred in your eyes.
They are co-joinèd halves that share each other's fate.
Love, hate, hate, love, each is a coin flipped twice.
That what is hate to me you may adore and love,
I may judge something wrong and call it vice,
Whereas for you it has a place in heav'n above.
I've often wondered about love and hate,
The games we play, the ever-present need for fight.
Could there be room for all in a debate?
Does sun make judgements about moon, does day judge night?
If we, with ease and grace, allowed all else to be,
There would be neither love nor hate, and we were free.

My Me

My Me inhabits many places
Depending where I walk in life
My love has many different faces

One of my redeeming graces
Is I am a friend to friends in strife
My Me inhabits many places

In different rhythms my heart races
As mother, daughter, lover, wife
My love has many different faces

Love is what interlaces
The various fabrics of my life
My Me inhabits many places

On odd occasions my love braces
Against the urge to wield a knife
My love has many different faces

I'd rather walk a thousand paces
Than stay the same when change is rife
My Me inhabits different places
My love has many different faces

My Right

I'm gonna stand tall
I'm gonna stand proud
I won't give a damn
I will not be cowed
I'm no longer afraid
To stand out from the crowd

I'm gonna speak up
I'm gonna speak out
I'm gonna make myself heard
I'm gonna cheer, sing and shout
I'm no longer scared
To face nerves, fear and doubt
I'm gonna explore
Try all sorts of things out
Learn from all my mistakes
That's what life is about

I will no longer walk
Hidden under a cloud
I'll let my light shine
And stand out from the crowd
I now claim my right
To stand tall, to stand proud

Never Mine

You were never mine
But you are mine to hold
And that must be enough

You were never mine
But you are mine to guide
And that must be enough

You were never mine
But you are mine to love
And that is enough

Dedicated to my beautiful children Tina and Phillip, of whom I could not be prouder.

Phoenix

Tears of despair
Irrigate
Burnt earth.

Tentative shoots
Test
Blackened soil.

Destruction
Delivers
A clean slate.

Loss of the old
Offers
New opportunities.

Out of the ashes
Rise
Bold beginnings.

Dedicated to the people affected by the South Australian Pinery fires in November 2015

Rich Beyond Belief

I am rich
Beyond belief
For I have loved.

Saturated

The smell of chasing birds across the blue.
The smell of a million scents in the sand.
The smell of seaweed and tide.

The smell of a tail held high.
The smell of muddy paws.
The smell of a voice hoarse from barking.

The smell of paw prints.
The smell of digging.
The smell of splashing.

The car is saturated with the smell of wet dog.

Oh Mother of Mine

Oh mother of mine, why are you so cruel,
So distant, disapproving, judgemental and cool?
All I've ever done was to follow my life,
Work, study, travel, never got into strife.
Got married, had children, brought them up right.
Instead of approval – accusation and fight.
You don't ask, you request. You don't give, only take.
There were times in my life, when I feared I would break.
You're a bottomless well, no matter how hard I try.
What you demand I simply cannot supply.
In your critical eyes I will never succeed.
So there's only one way, although it makes my heart bleed.
I have made up my mind. I will no longer stand by.
I have finally found strength. Please accept my good-bye.

The first line came to me after an argument with my mother. I extended the theme and put in all the grievances I could find, as you do… I might like to add that my mother and I are still on speaking terms.

Summer of Disobedience

1982
The summer of
My disobedience.

Backpack.
Train ticket.
Youth hostel pass.

Like time
I wait for
No one.

This poem goes back to a time when I was unhappily in love with an older man my parents vehemently disapproved of. As a consequence of the perpetual tension I decided to scout around Europe on my own for several months.

Summertime Wintertime

On warmer days we listen to the songbirds sing
And miss their cheerful voices in the months of frost.
We're made to change the dials to summertime in spring
Till autumn sees us gain the hour we deem lost.

Darkness we shift like bookends while we are asleep
So that our bodies may get used to time's new state.
We change the docile clocks like well-trained sheep,
Adjust without a fight to seasons' programmed fate.

To mourn the rising days' lost hour is in vain.
It gifts us with extended sunshine and more light
until in autumn clocks turn back and we regain
the missing minutes in the middle of the night.

But is time really simply one long linear line?
Is it a constant, never changing fixture set
In stone? Or is it fluid, willing to align
Itself with outcomes that intention may beget?

The change to summertime and the common phrase 'we're losing
an hour's sleep' made me think about the quality of time. Regulated
by the clock face, it seems a straightforward mathematical entity,
however, we all experience time at a different pace, and each one
of us has experienced time flying or time not wanting to pass.
Quantum physics tells us that atoms behave according to the
observer's intent. So what is time?

The Constancy of Change

When the time comes where you sense
With doubtless knowing and cloudless clarity
That something is coming to an end
Open your palms and let it go.

Life's only certainty is the constancy of change.
Let the universe fill your glass over and over again.
Drink every single drop.
For only what is empty can be filled.

The Crime of Ancestry

You came and you took me
In front of my wife
In front of my family
In the midst of my life

I have done nothing wrong
Except carry a name
You consider a threat
And feel free to defame

There's a war far away
Where we're fighting the Hun
But only Australians
Can carry a gun

I am willing to fight
I was born in this land
So just give me a gun
And I give you a hand

Instead you lock me away
You distrust and despise
Malign me and shame me
And choose to tell lies

So what chance have I got
To proof I stand fast
That only my name
Links me to the past

This is my home
This is where I belong
If you doubt my allegiance
You are very wrong

I have tended my vines
I have planted my wheat
For scores of years
I have worked in this heat

So don't tar me with guilt
Because of my name
It's not me, it's not us
It is you who's to blame

Maybe one day you will
Say sorry to me
And expunge the crime
Of my ancestry.

Inspired by Peter Goers and dedicated to all Australians of German ancestry who suffered persecution during World War I and II

The Cycle of Politics

Election
New beginning
Hope
Goodwill
Momentum
Proposals
Debate
Polarised policies
Factions fight
Like kids in a sandpit
Polished words of politics
Meandering answers
To straight questions
Little action
Lots of promises
No votable alternatives
Election

The Life That Could Have Been

You did what you thought best
Out of what you perceived as love
Guided by your need for respectability
You projected your fears
And your ideas of careers
And I
young and trained to please
Followed the markers you set
You knew no better
And meant well
I give you that
Blame has never altered anything
But in the silence of the night
I seek solace for my broken dreams
And mourn the life that could have been.

As I see it there are two ways of parenting. Acknowledging your children for who they are and supporting their decisions or moulding your children into what you think they should be and making their decisions for them. I would like to think that for the majority of my efforts as a parent I fall into the first category.

The Shell of Your Silence

Break the shell of your silence
Share your talents
Let everyone see what you have to contribute
Be noticed in all your glory.

You deserve attention.

Make this place a better place by being you
Stand in the light and make it brighter
Smile at the world
Let the world smile back at you.

You deserve to shine.

Show the world who you are
Be proud of where you come from
Find your power
Live your passion.

You deserve to be loved.

Inspired by Ana

The Silence Within

I listen to the mountains.
I listen to the stars.
I listen to the seas.
I listen to the desert.
I listen to the trees.

I listen
And find
The silence within.

This Is How

This is how I wish to die.
The silver cord that binds me to this body
Gets severed with a gentle sigh.
My consciousness starts lifting from this world.
My soul soars up towards the sky
Into the waiting arms of angels.
After an inner knowing made me say good-bye
To those I love and cherish
Only the dogs, sleeping close by,
Stir at the moment of my peaceful passing.
This is how I wish to die.

Three Wishes

If I had three wishes
I would that life would grant me these:

That I grow old with you
In comfortable silence
Forged by years of understanding.

That I see my children grow
And feel their children's arms
Soft around my neck.

That I gain in wisdom
See the world as it is
And still carry a lantern of hope.

I would that life would grant me these.

Tree Change

I am prepared to swap the seas
For the serenity of trees
and leave behind what I hold dear
For a new phase, a new career
I hope that by Life's care and grace
I will be guided to a place
Where I can let my soul run wild
And start again as if a child.

Some nights I lie awake with fear
I question why I can't stay here
But life tells me it's time for change
And everything that I arrange
Seems to be falling into place
I move along at this new pace
I feel excitement build inside
Let's just enjoy this crazy ride.

If I stay here I will grow old
I will forget how to be bold
If I stay here I will grow stale
Each day will put another nail
Into a coffin I designed
Because my life was not aligned
With what it had in store for me
So damn it, I will swap the sea.

Walk Through Doors That Open

Why worry
Which step to take
Which corner to turn
Which way to go

Walk through doors that open

Walking

I am walking on egg shells
Gauging his moods
Soothing his temper
Softening the blows
Pretending
That everything is all right
And maybe it is
It's usually my fault really
He doesn't mean it
But what happens to love
When only one does the holding
I am telling myself
That I am all right
But maybe I am not
It's not my fault really
I remember
Who I am
And I am walking out the door.

I was privileged to act in a TVC for the Zahra Foundation Australia, an organisation who 'supports women and their children to live a life free of violence and attain economic independence'. The experience inspired this poem which is dedicated to all the survivors of domestic violence.

Who Do You Think You Are

I am
An infinite being
Circling solar systems
And light
Each and every lifetime
I infuse myself
Into a new body
A new skin
A new colour
A new culture
A new world
I am
An infinite being
Of many shades
Forever changing
Forever the same.

Perfect

In a world of

Leaking taps
&
Squeaking hinges

ISIS
&
Brexit

Donald Trumps
&
Frank Underwoods

Syrias
&
Luke Batties

Mouse plagues
&
Bush fires

Your smile is perfect.

We Live, We Die

We live
We die
We fail
We try

We love
We hate
Destroy
Create

We plant
We grow
Reap as
We sow

We rhyme
We reason
We promise
We treason

We run
We walk
We silence
We talk

We doubt
We trust
We plan
We bust

We shout
We sing
Let go
And cling

We truth
We lie
We live
We die

www.ingramcontent.com/pod-product-compliance
Lightning Source LLC
Chambersburg PA
CBHW062203100526
44589CB00014B/1925